GEORGI

MW00902377

A Life From Beginning to End

Copyright © 2016 by Hourly History

Table of Contents

Introduction

A figure of both pride and controversy, General George S. Patton is frequently looked at as someone who was both crude and eloquent; heroic and outrageous. How did someone so iconic develop such a duality in common perception?

In truth, the strange dichotomy of General Patton seemed to begin when he was a small child. His duality of spirit was something that seemed to evolve as he listened to the nightly tales of his father and his war veteran friends. Hearing their stories of infantry charges and gallant bravery in the field, the young Patton began to dream and fantasize about himself filling their big shoes.

The power of his own imagination was so great that he could picture himself right there, fighting alongside his ancestors. This visual exercise would lead him to embrace the idea of reincarnation, beginning a lifelong belief that perhaps he had lived before, fighting on battlefields in the remote past.

In later years he was famously known for regaling his friends with suggestions of potential past lives he may have lived fighting for Rome's Legions, or as a trooper in Napoleon's artillery. However, regardless of his mystical leanings, whether he lived one life, or indeed a billion, his spirit was certainly larger than them all.

Chapter One

A Patent for Patton

"May God have mercy on my enemies, because I won't."

—General George S. Patton

The day that the great American General George S. Patton was born was not a day of particular significance. He arrived at the home of his already well-enshrined military family on November 11th, 1885 in San Gabriel, California. Twenty full years had passed since the close of the American Civil War, a conflict that had many of Patton's Virginia ancestors fighting for the losing side.

With this most deadly and disastrous of American wars two decades behind it, the country seemed to be relishing its newfound peace. Instead of fighting bloody wars and tearing the country apart, most American sentiment at this time was more focused on consolidating and conserving what they already had.

It was in 1885 that the Washington Monument was first dedicated, and it was also during this year that Niagara Falls State Park was established. In contrast to the severe discord the nation faced in 1865, in the year of Patton's birth, most Americans could perceive a general contentment and appreciation of what resources this nation—a little over a century old at this point—had to offer them.

But even though the world he was born into was at peace, it wasn't long before a young "Georgie," as his parents called him, began to look toward the devices of war. Growing up on ranches in Southern California, Patton's favorite pastime was to ride horses across the range, imagining himself leading brave cavalry charges against his enemies.

By the time Patton was 18, he would leave the ranches of California behind for the auspices of the Virginia Military Institute. which his forefathers had attended. His stay at VMI would be brief, however, and with the help of a letter of recommendation from Senator T.G. Bard of California, he would head straight to the most prestigious military training ground of all: West Point.

Initially, Patton seemed right at home on this hallowed ground of military training and appeared ready to excel. However, Patton would soon meet a foe he couldn't easily beat: mathematics. The future General who would storm through Europe against incredible odds was finding it difficult to calculate basic numeric equations. His grades were so bad he was forced to repeat his freshman year.

Through determined and intensive study during his summer break, however, the following year he was able to finally vanquish his mathematical nemesis once and for all. Patton would ultimately graduate from West Point on June 11th, 1909 ranked 46th in a class of 103. With his academic record intact, the world once again seemed ripe for George Patton to pick.

Immediately after his successful completion of his studies at West Point, Patton was able to realize his childhood dreams of riding across the plains on horseback when he was given the post of second lieutenant in the United States Cavalry, a field that would eventually lead him to his true destiny as a tank commander when horses would be phased out by mechanized warfare.

It was at this stage in Patton's life that he would find himself temporarily settling down, getting married and having children. He wed his longtime love, Beatrice Ayer, on May 26th, 1910 with whom he would have two daughters and one son. Then on September 1910 his military service would bring him to Fort Sheridan, just outside Chicago. It was here, just three years into his service, that Patton's life would take another sudden turn when his superiors selected him for—of all things—the Olympics of 1912.

At this point, the modern Olympic Games had only just been revived less than a decade before in 1896. Patton was given the honor of representing the United States in the fourth Olympics due to his excellent fencing and running ability, something that he was already well known for during his stint at West Point.

Three years after his exploits at the Olympics, in 1915 George Patton was transferred from Fort Sheridan to Fort Bliss, Texas, right across from the Mexican border. It was here that he became embroiled in border skirmishes between American troops and the Mexican bandits who frequently raided the border towns.

The situation on the border would become progressively more strained, culminating in March of 1916 when the Mexican General Pancho Villa sent about 100 of his fighters over the border to lay siege to the town of Columbus, New Mexico. It was in this surprise attack that Villa decimated the 13th Cavalry Regiment of the United States, stealing nearly 100 horses and a wide assortment of military equipment before burning the entire town to the ground.

To say that both the United States military and citizenry were shocked would be a massive understatement. This attack was the first major incursion on U.S. soil of a foreign power since the British attacked in 1812, and an instance of outside aggression that would not be repeated again until the Japanese bombed Hawaii on December 7th, 1941.

Having that said, the U.S. government took this raid very seriously. As a result, the then President Woodrow Wilson ordered 5000 U.S. troops to cross the border and capture Pancho Villa. General John Pershing was commissioned to lead this charge, and it was Pershing who soon afterward recruited George Patton to assist him in the effort, eventually making him an integral part of the 13th Cavalry, the very unit that had been sacked by Pancho Villa.

It was here that Patton would have his first foray into combat when on May 14th, 1916 he took ten soldiers and two civilian scouts in three Dodge touring cars over the Mexican border. It didn't take Patton long to find his target, as he and his men quickly located and overtook a group of Villa's militants, killing three of them in the process. This gained Patton some immediate notoriety in the press, who began to call him the "bandit killer."

Despite this early success against Villa's bandits, Pancho Villa himself remained at large; the expedition was called off in February of 1917. Patton didn't have to sit idle for long, however, because the winds of change were blowing in Europe and a series of events would soon launch half of the planet into World War One.

It was here that Patton's old mentor Pershing was commissioned as the commander of the AEF (American Expeditionary Force) in the conflict. Following in Pershing's footsteps, Patton was soon sent to the Western Front to join him on May 15th, 1917. It was here that Patton would first come acquainted with the newly-minted mechanized military behemoth known as the tank.

During his time in Europe, he actually attended a French Tank school, expanding his knowledge and excitement on the subject exponentially. Patton's interest in tanks would soon pay off when he was given the post of first officer within the United States' own recently established Tank Corps. Patton soon became an expert in tank maintenance and strategy.

After World War One came to a close, Patton's beloved Tank Corps was temporarily disbanded, but not before Patton made the request to his superiors—should the corps ever return—that he would be placed at its head. This was a request that would inevitably launch Patton into the history books again decades later when yet another world war, even more ferocious than the first, would embroil the globe.

Chapter Two

In Between War

"A pint of sweat will save a gallon of blood."

—General George S. Patton

For George S. Patton, life in between the battlements of war was a battle in itself. Never one wanting to be idle during peacetime, Patton dove headlong into a wide assortment of posts, assignments, and enterprises. Most notably, in 1920 he worked on a project in Washington D. C. to write one of the first user guides in the form of instruction manuals on operating military tanks.

It was during this period that Patton first became acquainted with future General, and future President, Dwight D. Eisenhower. The two soon developed a bond that would last the rest of Patton's life. Besides Eisenhower, during the interwar period, Patton met many that would prove integral in shaping his later career. However, despite his success in climbing the social ladder of his professional circle, Patton soon became incredibly weary of the life of a peacetime staff officer.

He would soon welcome an escape from all of the D.C. political hobnobbing and intrigue he was surrounded with when he was redeployed to Hawaii in 1925. By all accounts, the Pattons fell in love with life on the Hawaiian Islands, and it was a great time for them to reconnect with each other as a family. General George Patton's son in particular would recall, years later and with much fondness, how he and his father would scour the beaches flying model airplanes and their long excursions in the ocean.

All good things must come to an end, however, and the Patton family, just a few years later, were given the marching orders to return back to Washington in 1928. Back in D.C. once again Patton was given the designation as "Chief of Cavalry," a position that took up quite a bit of Patton's time, going from one location to another overseeing the units of which he was in charge.

It was in this role of overseer that Patton sought to pick up where he left off when it came to merging mechanized warfare with the more traditional cavalry brigades. He sought to merge artillery, infantry, and cavalry all in one heavily mechanized unit. He was initially given free reign to experiment with his concept, but due to a sudden cut in funding from the U.S. Congress, Patton had to abandon his plans.

With his plans temporarily scuttled, life for Patton took on a rather mundane routine. In the next few years, the only respite from his peacetime malaise came in the form of a massive protest of veterans marching on the capital in the summer of 1932. The disgruntled vets, who were known as the "Bonus Expeditionary Force" in mock sarcasm of the American Expeditionary Force they served in during World War One, were unemployed and demanding compensation.

In 1924 many of them had been awarded certificates that guaranteed them future bonus payments that could be redeemed by the year 1945. Most of these veterans, suffering miserably from the Great Depression of the 1930s, were fed up; not wanting to wait another decade for their promised commission, they took to the streets to demand immediate cash payment for the money that they had been promised.

Most of these men most likely served right alongside Patton on the Western Front, and he no doubt had sympathy for their cause, but ever the resolute soldier, he couldn't disobey his orders. On July 28th, he cast whatever sympathy for his former brothers in arms aside and led a charge against the protesters, driving them away from the White House with bayonets and tear gas.

Concerning the event, Patton would later admit that he was disgusted with the treatment of the veterans but acknowledged that it was a necessary evil at the time in order to prevent what he feared would become an "armed insurrection" against the United States government. Patton's strict obedience to these tough directives would soon pay off in 1934 when he was given the rank of a Lieutenant Colonel and soon afterward sent back to his beloved Hawaii.

It was here that he began to have a keen interest once again in the international affairs that were shaping the globe. From the vantage point of Hawaii, in particular, he began to keep a close watch on developments across the Pacific with the ever-expanding power of Japan.

Incredibly, Patton—the astute military analyst—even seemed to predict Pearl Harbor years in advance in a document he composed under the heading "Surprise," which laid out in detail his theory of how easily the Japanese could (and probably would) conduct a surprise attack on the Hawaiian Islands. Even in between war, the mind of General George Patton was prophetic and profound.

Chapter Three

This Means War

"Duty is but discipline carried to its highest degree."

—General George S. Patton

Although the Pattons were no longer stationed in Hawaii on December 7th, 1941 when the Japanese launched a massive surprise attack on Pearl Harbor, in the words of President Franklin Delano Roosevelt, it certainly was a day that would "live in infamy." Just a few months prior to this infamous date, George S. Patton would finally attain the title of General, first as a Brigadier General on October 2nd, 1941 and then as a Major General on April 4th, 1941.

Even before the Japanese attack, the whole country seemed to be abuzz with rumors of war as the entire nation watched very closely the events transpiring between the fascist Axis powers, of Germany, Japan, and Italy. Beyond the fear and speculation of the general public, for the United States Military, war seemed like a very real possibility, one way or another.

About one year prior to Pearl Harbor in December 1940, Patton had famously conducted a massive mock run of 1000 tanks from Columbus, Georgia all the way to Panama City, Florida. This was the practice drill for the incredible drive that General Patton would ultimately lead his tank battalions through in France just a few years later.

However, the site of General Patton's first land invasion would not be Europe; it would be Africa. It was in the summer of 1942 that General Dwight D. Eisenhower assigned Patton to the liberation of North Africa under the codename "Operation Torch." The force that Patton led was composed of 33,000 men landing on the shores of Casablanca in about 100 various landing ships.

They arrived on November 8th, 1942, where they were met with a fairly stiff opposition by the Nazi-orchestrated French forces of the "Vichy" puppet government that the Germans had installed shortly after France's Nazi occupation. Regardless of the enemies' ferocity, however, Patton made short work of them, managing to take out Casablanca and negotiate an armistice on November 11th, 1942.

Patton couldn't have been happier; Casablanca would be taken completely intact without another shot needing to be fired, and to top it all off it was the old General's birthday; he took the armistice as the best birthday gift he could have had. The Moroccan port of Casablanca was quickly transformed into a military base, hosting the Casablanca Conference two months later.

It was during this conference that the combined Chiefs of Staff directed the plans of what would be the invasion of Sicily, striking out directly at the Italian sphere of influence and beginning the liberation of Europe. However, before Europe could be taken, the battle for North Africa had to be completed, and after Operation Torch had run its course, the next chapter of that mission began in the Tunisian campaign in a place called the Kasserine Pass in February of 1943.

Locked within the famous range of the Atlas Mountains, German General Erwin Rommel led his Afrika Korps with a combined regiment of Italian Tanks and two Panzer divisions against the Allied advance. The Allied forces for their part were extremely ill-prepared and inexperienced in this offensive and were easily pushed back by Rommel's forces.

Realizing that the deck needed to be shuffled, military high command sought to replace the inexperienced leadership with none other than General George S. Patton. All American units in Tunisia were placed under his direct command in March of 1943. Even though Patton had already proved himself during the siege of Casablanca, his new charges' first reaction to him were mixed at best.

During an introductory convocation to his new troops, he was perceived by these already battle-tested veterans as profane and obscene. Many who had just tasted the bitterness of war for the first time stared in disbelief as Patton assured them of the "glory of death" on the battlefield. Patton's grim encouragement that these men should fight until the "tank was shot out from under them" and even then keep on fighting "on foot" was like salt in being sprinkled in their still-fresh wounds.

Instead of these calls to arms rallying their spirits, many of these already battle-hardened men just felt taken advantage of. As one of the soldiers of the time described the sentiment, those who heard Patton's harangue about the glory of shedding blood and having guts felt they were the ones that would "provide the blood" while Patton would "provide the guts." Incidentally enough this was where General Patton received the nickname that would follow him throughout the rest of the war: "Old Blood and Guts."

Despite some of the initial criticism his spirited persona brought upon him, Patton was given clear instructions: he was ordered to turn around a defeated and demoralized battalion within 10 days. This may have seemed like a monumental task for some, but for Patton, it was just a matter of protocol. He approached the faltering unit with a bottom-up approach.

Wanting to give the whole group a complete facelift, and with the apparent opinion that a well-dressed soldier is a much more confident soldier, he replaced their dirty and blood-stained clothing with fresh, clean, and neatly pressed uniforms. He then started drilling them around the clock according to his own breakneck routine.

He brought these veterans of the conflict back to square one, hitting the reset button. For those ten days, he brought them right back to boot camp so he could personally see their strengths and weaknesses and then use all the knowledge at his disposal to mold them into a more effective fighting machine. This was Patton 101, and he expected them to pass his 10-day crash course with flying colors.

The final exam for his lesson plan was an uphill charge against the enemy position of Gafsa in Tunisia. General Patton wouldn't be disappointed, and on March 17th, 1943, in the Battle of El Guettar, they drove the Italian and German divisions out. For Patton, this was the entrance he needed for the true stepping stone to Europe: Sicily.

Chapter Four

Operation Husky

"The object of war is not to die for your country but to make the other bastard die for his."

—General George S. Patton

General Patton and a force of 90,000 men converged on the Sicilian beach town of Licata on July 10th, 1943. The battalion was highly effective, securing the beachfront almost immediately while beating back joint German and Italian attacks. The fascists were eventually driven to the sea, and at the end of the battle, with only 7,500 American casualties compared to the 113,000 enemy troops that were neutralized, it would appear to be another stunning success story of General Patton's command.

With such a stunning victory, Patton quickly consolidated his grip on the island while the surviving German and Italian forces (about 100,000 in all) fled to Italy. With the enemy on the run, it gave Patton's weary troops time to rest and Patton time to consider his next move. However, even with his Axis adversaries on the run, Patton's long-time enemy of controversy wasn't far behind.

Soon, several events would erupt on the Sicilian Island that would turn into a public relations nightmare. The first bad precedent that Patton set was when he mercilessly shot and killed two mules and then beat their complaining owner with a stick! Apparently, the poor Sicilian farmer had temporarily lost control of the farm animals, and they found themselves on a bridge when Patton's armored column approached. Like deer caught in headlights, the farm animals seemed just to freeze in place, completely blocking the path of Patton's unit.

Never one much for patience, after screaming and cursing, Patton pulled out his gun and started shooting. That's when the owner, who was trying to corral the animals, popped up and began to lament bitterly over what Patton had done. It's unsure if Patton even knew what the poor man was saying, but not liking the overall sound and tone of the man's cries, Patton decided to take out a walking stick and start beating him with it.

After the man ran for cover, Patton then kicked his dead animals off the bridge and ordered his men to move forward. One can only speculate if this unfortunate fellow had previously welcomed his liberation from the Italian dictator Benito Mussolini, but sadly, after experiencing such ruthlessness from the United States military, it's safe to say that he may have had some second thoughts.

However, it wasn't only the native Sicilians that bore the brunt of Patton's heavy-handedness - it was often his own men that were dealt blows from his iron fist, as was quite literally the case in the infamous slapping incidents of Private's Charles H. Kuhl and Paul G. Bennet. These men had clear cases of battle fatigue, or what we would call Post Traumatic Stress Disorder (PTSD) today.

No matter how shell-shocked these troubled soldiers appeared in their hospital beds, Patton wasn't buying any of it. On two separate occasions visiting them, he slapped them both in the face and denounced them as nothing more than complaining cowards. Having never experienced it himself, Patton obviously refused to believe in the veracity of claims of war wrought mental disturbances such as PTSD, and felt that he could somehow snap (or slap!) the frazzled infantrymen out of it.

The nearby doctors who witnessed the event didn't take too kindly to this rampaging General so casually assaulting their patients, though, and once the violent episodes reached the ears of General Dwight D. Eisenhower, Patton was told to stand down and was even forced to apologize. As much as high command wanted Patton to make amends for his misdeeds, however, they also sought to cover for him, dreading the idea of such wanton violations of power reaching the media.

Despite the efforts to quash the story, the event still managed to leak out and was making headlines back in America by November 1943. As a result of all this bad publicity Patton was kicked to the sidelines for nearly a whole year. For the most part, Patton was dealt with rather lightly, considering that the typical rigid protocol of the United States Military under normal circumstances would have sought an immediate court-martial against Patton.

In the end, it was sheer necessity that kept Eisenhower from taking more severe action against him. General

Patton was his best eyes and ears on the field, and as outrageous as his behavior was, the Allied effort could not afford to lose him. Even so, it wouldn't be until January 26th that he would be given a chance to redeem himself, with a new post in England preparing for what would be the biggest battle of his career: the invasion of Normandy.

Chapter Five

Invasion of Normandy

"I am a soldier, I fight where I am told, and I win where I fight."

—General George S. Patton

After quietly being whisked away to England while his latest battlefield controversy was allowed to dissipate, Patton was given charge of a new army, poised and ready to make history like never before. The United States "Third Army," a mechanized battalion made to be as mobile as possible, this fighting unit was scheduled to come crashing right through continental Europe in July of 1944.

The original architects of the blitzkrieg, the Germans, feared the threat of Patton's own lightning-fast assault more than anyone else. During the summer months of 1944 all German eyes were kept steadily trained on General Patton, so much so that U.S. military intelligence conceived of a brilliant ploy to throw the Germans off balance.

Even though the planned invasion had always been meant to be on the western shores of France at Normandy, the U.S. began a concerted effort to send misinformation and false intelligence reports to German operatives that the planned invasion would be for Pas de Calais in the North of France instead.

This Allied campaign of deception even went so far as to create a so-called "phantom army" in which they used Hollywood-style props of fake boats and planes that they amassed on the British coastline of Dover just parallel to Pas de Calais across the English Chanel. Dover, in southeast England, would have been the closest launching point, and the most obvious choice for an invasion of France, but the German high command should have realized that this choice was a bit too obvious for the Americans ever actually to consider it.

Continuing their ruse however under the moniker of "Operation Fortitude," General Patton was told to keep a low profile while fake armaments were positioned all over the Dover coast so that German officials would indeed believe that their dreaded adversary was planning an invasion from the Southeast Corner of England to Pas de Calais.

In the end the ploy worked perfectly; the Axis was so convinced that an invasion of Pas de Calais was imminent that even after Patton and his men landed in Normandy some 150 miles away, the Nazis refused to reinforce the position and kept their battalions fully in place, facing off against the phantom army that never came.

Patton's army made its first landings in July and was operational on the mainland by August 1st, 1944. It was an assault in which Patton was determined to use speed and aggressiveness to his full advantage. One of Patton's main strategies was to send scout units ahead of the main army and use them to probe the enemy's weaknesses; he would then send "self-propelled artillery" to move in on these sites as the rest of the armored column advanced.

The only problem was the fact that the whole German army was so well camouflaged in the French terrain that whole German units would often blend in and disappear right in the middle of a French farm or hedgerow. With the Germans keeping their major army hidden until nightfall, a kind of constant game of cat and mouse developed between German convoys and the Allied Air Force that wished to obliterate them.

Even more deadly were the sniper posts and pill boxes scattered all over the countryside in which expert German marksman could remain safe from the fray, high up in trees with cleverly camouflaged ladders available for a quick escape, while they rained down death from above. Despite these obstacles, however, Patton's men marched on in quick succession.

This rapid advance would continue until August 31st, 1944, when his Third Army's tanks were faced with a fuel shortage on the outskirts of the town of Metz. According to those who witnessed it, Patton's tanks, trucks, and jeeps all, one by one, simply coasted to a halt as each vehicle quite literally ran out of gas. The infantry was immediately ordered out of the trucks they had been riding in and began to walk on foot.

Patton, surveying the disastrous fuel shortage, began sending a flurry of telegrams to Eisenhower, demanding to know why he wasn't given enough gasoline to complete his mission. He reportedly told Eisenhower that "his men would willingly go without food, and even ammunition, if they could just have oil."

Many hungry soldiers would probably beg to differ with the statement made on their behalf, but Patton's proposition of food for oil would fall on deaf ears anyway; High Command had other plans with their preciously-allocated resources and allowing Patton another gallant charge was not one of them. Being cut off from a fuel supply, Patton had no choice but to park his tanks and have his men dig in their heels, fortifying the ground they already had as they busied themselves making fortifications on wide swaths of land from Luxembourg to Nancy.

For the moment, Patton's advance was ground to a halt. Some believed that Eisenhower purposefully limited Patton's fuel just to keep some control over the wild general. Fearing that if Old Blood and Guts had enough fuel, he wouldn't stop until he drove to Berlin and beyond—a feat that the Allied Command wasn't quite ready for—so it was decided to pull the plug on the brash General early.

This momentary cessation in fighting, however, was enough to allow the local German forces to recalibrate and fortify their positions. And as a result, throughout all of October and November, when Patton's Third Army finally engaged the armed fortifications in Metz, it was largely a stalemate with major casualties on both sides of the conflict.

Patton temporarily stalled, then sent his forces to try and overrun Fort Driant to the south of Metz, but the invasion force was soundly knocked back by the fanatically defending Germans. With long guns blazing through impenetrable concrete, Patton's men couldn't make any headway. After losing six tanks, 50 men, and having over 300 more wounded, Patton cut his losses and abandoned the attempt on Fort Driant, dismissing his failure as a simple "engineering experiment which did not work."

At any rate, the capture of Fort Driant was a fairly meaningless exercise with no vital strategic importance. Patton realized this fact, conceding to the Germans, who were already trapped and entombed like the dead inside their massive concrete fort. He moved on, he and his men slowly making their march west.

Chapter Six

The Battle of the Bulge

"Lead me, follow me, or get out of my way."

—General George S. Patton

The Battle of the Bulge was Germany's last gasp of an attempt to alter the course of the war. With heavy losses in the east against the Russians and the fast approaching Allies in the West, Germany was being quickly pressured from two different directions. The Battle of the Bulge was a last-ditch effort to escape the vise that Germany was being squeezed with.

On December 16th, 1944, German tanks and artillery that had been previously hidden deep in the Ardennes Forest were sent out of their hiding places in a furious drive to meet the American army head on. An emergency meeting was called by Eisenhower, in which he met with Patton and several other Generals and officers to assess the situation.

Attention quickly turned to Patton as Eisenhower asked him how long it would take him to muster an effective counterattack against the German assault. Patton wasted no time with his answer, as he responded declaratively, "as soon as you're through with me." Eisenhower scoffed at this assertion as more of Patton's empty boasting and insisted that he wait until a few days later on December 22nd when his men could be better prepared to face the oncoming German threat.

When Patton left this conference, he immediately called up his command staff and famously instructed them, "play ball." These were the preordained code words that Patton had instructed his staff to follow before he met with Eisenhower that signaled them to immediately begin mobilizing and preparing for the counter-offensive against the Germans.

It was the day after Christmas; December 26th, that Patton's army met up with the resurgent Germans. At first Patton's men were dug down deep in their positions doing all they could to avoid enemy fire, but soon it came to be the Germans' turn to be used for target practice as their infantry attempted a daring charge out of the forest at the Allied line.

The weather was against them, and being knee-deep in snow, their charge soon turned into a shuffle through the elements that bogged them down. It became quite easy for Patton's men to pick off these Germans practically swimming in the snow. They tried again and again, and each time was met with deadly results at the hands of Patton's army.

Soon they were in full retreat, and Patton reached the bombed-out town of Bastogne to open up a corridor to relieve the beleaguered U.S. battalions that had been trapped there. With the daring rescue of these previously ensnared souls, the Battle of the Bulge was over, and the Germans were once again sent packing back across the Rhine.

On March 22nd, Patton finally gave chase by having his engineers build a pontoon bridge over the Rhine. At this point, Patton was taking his time, and supposedly even urinated right into the river as he walked across. At first, it seemed like clear sailing for the men of Patton's Third Army, but as the hours wore on, his men marching across the Rhine were eventually spotted by what was left of the German Air Force.

Shortly thereafter, some of the few remaining Messerschmitt fighters from the Luftwaffe started vigorously harassing Patton's approaching columns of soldiers. The German pilots would fly daringly low and then dive at the approaching troops while unleashing their aircraft's machine guns.

The maneuver ended up costing the German pilots much more than any casualty inflicted upon Patton's battalion, however; amazingly, all 33 of the attacking Messerschmitt fighters that day were shot out of the sky by the Third Army's highly effective anti-aircraft weaponry.

After their path had been cleared for them, Patton began to formulate their next move. Thinking that momentum was on their side and they now had the time and resources to do it, Patton set his sights on a nearby POW camp and hatched a plot to free the inmates. On March 26th, 1945, Patton convened what would become known as "Task Force Baum," named after the 23-year-old Captain Abraham J. Baum whom Patton had commissioned to lead the mission.

This task force of would-be liberators was made up of 16 tanks and 314 men. Many warned Patton that 314 soldiers were not enough to take such a heavily fortified compound, but ever willing to test his luck (and the patience of others), Patton launched the daring mission anyway. Task Force Baum was sent some 50 miles behind enemy lines in order to free detainees from the fortified prisoner of war camp on the outskirts of Hammelburg.

As many of his detractors had feared, the German opposition dug into this compound was fierce; nearly half of the men that comprised Task Force Baum were killed in their first approach. Even worse, once the remaining members of the task force managed to storm through the main gate, due to a combination of fatigue and personal ignorance they mistook several Serbian prisoners still wearing their military uniforms to be guards and inadvertently massacred many of them.

The bloodshed was only put to a stop when one of the actual Germans in charge of guarding the compound, General Gunther Von Guckel, who felt sorry for the Serbs who were being butchered by the Americans, instructed some of his American POWs to confront the task force's confused participants and explain to them the situation.

While the American POW's managed to fill in the details, General Gunther and most of the other German guards took the opportunity to flee from the compound altogether. The task force didn't bother pursuing them and instead focused on the goal of freeing the prisoners. It was then that they found General Patton's main objective in creating this mission; Patton's son-in-law Colonel Waters.

Running to them through the front gate with a white flag of surrender in his hand, and flanked by one of the few remaining German officers, it was supposed to be Task Force Baum's moment of triumph in which they could report back to Patton that they had succeeded in rescuing the Colonel, let alone the hundreds of other detainees they freed.

However, as fate would have it, matters would take a turn for the worst as bullets ripped out of nowhere from one remaining German guard who had been camouflaged in the background, hiding and waiting. The Colonel only received a flesh wound and would survive, but the injury rendered him unable to walk, creating yet another liability for the mission.

The most glaring problem of all, however, was the sheer number of prisoners they had rescued, miscalculating how many POWs were actually imprisoned at the camp. The task force quickly realized that their vehicles had nowhere near the capacity to transport all of them. In their first attempt, they had to cram over 700 people in and on top of several tanks and trucks.

It was in this state of burdensome disarray that the German army caught them and led a vicious counterattack. Picking the hapless prisoners right out of the vehicles, the Germans viciously reclaimed their POWs and even added more to their collection from the failed rescuers of Task Force Baum.

In the end, of all the brave souls who staged this rescue, only 35 made it back with their lives. The mission was a complete failure. In later testimony, Patton would claim that his failure to liberate this one POW camp was the only mistake that he made during the course of the entire war. A great testament to his skill; by Germany's surrender on May 9th, 1945, Old Blood and Guts' battle record was otherwise impeccable.

Chapter Seven

An Old Man's War

"Anyone in any walk of life who is content with mediocrity is untrue to himself and to American tradition."

—George S. Patton

In the spring of 1945, most Americans were rather optimistic about the future. Their war effort in both the armaments factories at home and the battlefields abroad seemed to be fruitful and paying massive dividends. America had stood up to the most ruthless dictatorial power the world had ever known and was not only successful but seemed poised for a major victory.

The last thing they expected to hear in what should have been a national moment of triumph was the death of the political figure who led them there. It came as an incredible shock to all who heard it on April 12th of 1945 when word spread of President Franklin Delano Roosevelt's death. F.D.R.—as many liked to call him—had been part the American consciousness for many years.

In fact, F.D.R. was the only United States President to be elected 4 times, which led to the standard 2-term limit for U.S. presidents in the future. It is fair to say that F.D.R. and his fireside chats were quite imprinted on the minds of all Americans at that point. He was not only the commander-in-chief for the United States during World War Two, but he also led the country through the horrible economic downturn of the Great Depression and every other national crisis of the last two decades.

For his part, General George S. Patton was just as shocked to hear the news anyone else. As prophetic as his words had been in the past over other issues, he really did not see this one coming. That very same day he had been touring the horrors of newly freed concentration camps where the blood of recently executed victims—stacked neatly like pieces of wood in the corner—still dripped onto the floors.

The shock of all these grisly sights was then enhanced later that day when Patton learned about the demise of his President, a man that he genuinely admired. By all accounts this admiration was reciprocal, with F.D.R. often fondly referring to Patton as "Old Cavalryman" and even on occasion remarking that Patton was "Our Greatest Fighting General."

Patton was filled with grief to hear of the loss of a man he greatly respected while simultaneously being filled with doubt at the thought of his successor—a man he held in little esteem—Harry S. Truman, taking over the final days of the war effort. Shortly after he received word of the President's demise, Patton was ordered to attend a meeting with his immediate superiors, General Omar Bradley and General Dwight Eisenhower.

Of all places to meet, they had chosen an abandoned salt mine that Patton's men had discovered just days before. The mine had been used by the Nazis as a last minute hideaway to hoard millions of dollars in currency, gold bars, and famous works of art. Eisenhower wanted to survey the buried treasure with his Generals before he decided what to do with it.

As the rickety wooden elevator took them down to the deep dark depths below, Patton was as macabre as ever as he pointed out the precarious nature of the thin rope the three men's elevator descended on. He sarcastically quipped, "if that clothesline breaks, promotions in the United States Army should be considerably stimulated!"

Eisenhower wasn't in the mood for his absurd humor, however, and quickly shut down the old General with, "George, that's enough! No more wisecracks until we are above ground!" All jokes aside, as Patton continued to stare out at the thin silver cord that their elevator was hanging from, he knew that it served all too well to represent the precarious state which they were all in.

Even though they had won the war, their President was dead and now three of the most powerful men in the United States military, one of them a future president himself, were miles deep under the German ground lost in an ever-increasing fog of darkness. All of these grim details seemed to perfectly set the mood of the post-World War Two World that would follow.

Chapter Eight

Watch Your Mouth

"Moral courage is the most valuable and usually the most absent characteristic in men."

—General George S. Patton

As World War Two came to a close and the lines of Europe were beginning to be drawn, Patton could clearly see the fractured lines of the Allies begin to emerge as well. Even as the Germans were surrendering, Patton knew that the next threat wouldn't be from Germany - it would be from Russia and its ideology of communist world domination.

However, Dwight D. Eisenhower had his own fears, and more than Russia he feared an unreserved General Patton creating a diplomatic disaster on the world stage. Seeking to preoccupy the outspoken General from his idle political intrigue, Eisenhower sent Patton to be the Military Governor of Bavaria, far removed from the other international players of the post-war peace.

Shipped off quietly to a Bavarian villa where he would have his own swimming pool, bowling alley, and even two yachts, it was hoped that the conqueror of Western Europe would be preoccupied enough to keep his mouth shut. However, as he looked over the Bavarian hills,

Patton still longed for one more battle while his army was at full strength.

For a time Patton toyed with the idea of seeking a transfer to the Pacific so he could at least ride out the last conflict in the still-raging war against the Japanese. However, even more than this, Patton continued to suggest—what was at the time unthinkable—that the United States should militarily engage their supposed eastern ally, the Russians.

This was before the Cold War and before the Iron Curtain descended upon Europe. At this point in time, official U.S. policy was that "Russia was our friend," and anyone that had reservations about the relationship was to keep them to themselves. To the chagrin of Eisenhower and the rest of the high command, Patton refused to toe this line.

Without holding back, or any sense of political tact, he is reported to have openly told journalists in regard to the relations with the Russians, "you cannot lay down with a diseased jackal. Neither can we ever do business with the Russians. Let's keep our boots polished, bayonets sharpened, and present a picture of force and strength to these people.

"This is the only language they understand and respect. If you fail to do this, then I would like to say to you that we have had a victory over the Germans but have lost the war." When Patton's latest slip of the mouth reached Eisenhower, he was furious, believing that such statements were provocative and potentially dangerous incitements to a nation he still hoped would be a potential ally and partner in the peace process.

Eisenhower wished to keep the Russians from hearing such combative rhetoric out of his Generals, but according to some reports, the Kremlin was well aware of Patton's criticisms of their government; as a result, it had landed this American General on the watch list of the notorious NKVD. Shortly after this Russian surveillance of Patton began, he was personally visited by a Russian General at his Bavarian headquarters.

Coming completely unannounced, the Russian Field Marshal General was escorted into Patton's office by his surprised Chief of Staff. After a brief introduction, the Russian General then issued Patton a series of demands and criticisms of how his men have conducted themselves. A particular point of concern was the fact that so many Germans had been allowed to flee the Russians and seek refuge in the American sector of the occupation.

This was quite a common occurrence since the Germans knew that the Americans' treatment of them would be much more humane than the revenge-seeking Russians, who were already well known for their brutality against German citizens. In particular, the Russian General raised the issue of German boatmen who were using their ships to ferry hundreds of German refugees across the Danube and into the safety of the American Zone.

The Russian General then went on to assert that these boats and their operators were the property of the Russians since they were coming out of the Russian Zone, and as a consequence demanded that Patton have these men and their boats turned back over to the Russians at once. Patton's Chief of Staff recalls the deafening silence in the room after the ultimatum was made.

Patton, not saying a word, coldly stared at the Russian General as he slowly, painstakingly, took the Cuban cigar he had been smoking out of his mouth and placed it in his ashtray. His eyes still staring emotionlessly at the Russian before him, he then quietly opened his desk drawer as he pulled out his specially made Smith and Wesson .357 revolver.

As both the Russian General and Patton's Chief of Staff stared in shock, Patton then slammed the revolver down on his desk, his formerly placid face erupting in fury as he screamed, "get this son of a bitch out of here! Who in the hell let him in? Don't let any more Russian bastards into this headquarters!" He then turned to his Chief of Staff and quickly rattled off in frenzied fury, "Alert the Fourth and Eleventh and Sixty-Fifth Divisions for an attack to the east!"

At this point even the hardened Russian General looked terrified, truly believing that General Patton had just signed off on World War Three. Trembling as Patton's Chief of Staff quickly led him out of the room, the previously imposing Field Marshal from the East was, by all accounts, scared to death.

But as insane as the theatrics were, they had all failed to call the General's bluff. When the Chief of Staff returned, fearing that they were on the verge of all-out war with Russia, he was puzzled to find the previously enraged Patton, completely relaxed with a satisfied smile on his face. He asked, "How was that?"

As his Chief of Staff could only stare in stunned silence, Patton answered for him as he continued, "sometimes you have to put on an act, and I'm not going to let any Russian marshal, general, or private tell me what I have to do." Patton then nonchalantly added, "call off the alert, that's the last we'll hear from those bastards." This was, in fact, the last time Patton would be questioned by the Russians; in just a few months, he would be dead.

Chapter Nine

Man of Controversy

"Say what you mean, and mean what you say."

—General George S. Patton

General George S. Patton was a man that spoke his mind and usually invited much controversy upon himself in the process. Many viewed his capacity as a so-called "straight shooter" to be his best asset and also his worst detriment. There can be no doubt the worst of Patton's tirades came when he belittled the very people he worked so hard to save - the Nazi Holocaust survivors.

As Governor of Bavaria, Patton was in charge of the displaced persons who survived the camps. Patton would come to frequently make known the displeasure he often felt for the Jews, Gypsies, Russians, Hungarians, and Poles that he was in charge of. He once even made the ridiculous observation that the displaced people in his charge dressed in filthy rags and smelled bad.

Anyone with a little common sense, of course, would realize that after spending months or even years in a concentration camp, deprived of even the most basic necessities, hygiene would not be the greatest of priorities. No doubt the fact that the displaced individuals put under his care were still wearing the filthy prisoner uniforms that the Nazis had given them was a fact that you could only blame General Patton for.

While he was indignantly complaining about how unbecoming the detainees appeared, he was actually the one who was depriving them of having fresh clothing. This belligerent absurdity displayed by Patton toward the very people he rescued was just the tip of the iceberg, however. Soon Patton would bring his deeply-held disdain and contempt right out in the open.

On one occasion in particular, Eisenhower—most likely seeking to bridge the cultural divide between Patton and his detainees—took the General to a synagogue on Yom Kippur. The General behaved himself for the most part, but Patton would later remark, "we entered the synagogue, which was packed with the greatest stinking mass of humanity I have ever seen. Of course, I have seen them since the beginning and marvelled that beings alleged to be made in the form of God can look the way they do or act the way they act."

Patton's comments are disgusting in the extreme, and it is hard for most to imagine that the same man viewed by so many as the gallant liberator of Europe could say such horrible things. His cruelty doesn't end with his words; Patton was also eventually highly criticized for housing former Nazis in the same DP camps as Holocaust survivors.

Even worse than this, there is evidence of Patton giving former Nazis—the very people that he had rescued the other displaced persons from—preferential treatment and in some cases even giving them special supervisory roles over others in the camp. Things became so bad that you couldn't blame Holocaust survivors for believing that they had simply been liberated from a German-styled concentration camp to a General George Patton American-styled one.

As word of the poor treatment of the refugees at Patton's DP camps spread, outside activists began to speak out. Gaining the ear of newly elected President Harry Truman, a special envoy headed by former immigration official Earl Harrison was sent to inspect Patton's camps. They were appalled to find the complaints about the treatment of refugees were, in fact, well-founded.

After a scathing report was sent back to D.C., Patton's actions were immediately called into question and measures were taken to improve the lives of the detained refugees. For his part, the only explanation that Patton could give for treating the displaced persons in his camp more like prisoners under armed guard than liberated citizens was supposedly for their own protection.

According to Patton, he made the claim that, if the displaced persons (DPs) "were not kept under guard they would not stay in the camps, would spread over the country like locusts, and would eventually have to be rounded up after quite a few of them had been shot and quite a few Germans murdered and pillaged."

As dark and disturbing as the imagery that Patton espoused could be, this was his defense. He claimed that he was saving the DPs as well as the average German citizen, believing that if Holocaust survivors were allowed to roam free, chaos would erupt and they may be targeted by angry Germans and in turn, the DPs may seek revenge attacks on average German citizens, robbing and killing them at will.

This was Patton's rationale for keeping thousands of people under barbed wire and armed guard 24 hours a day. However, Eisenhower wasn't buying it; on September 28th, 1945 he officially relieved Patton from his Military Governorship of Bavaria. About a week later, on October 7th, he then completely removed Patton from his position of leadership over the entire Third Army.

Patton was then transferred to the Fifteenth United States Army, which was a small office staff who spent their time compiling a history of the war in Europe. At first, Patton was somewhat satisfied with the assignment because of his professed love of history, but without any direct action, he quickly became bored and restless.

During these last few months of his life, he began to roam about aimlessly in Western Europe, visiting Paris on occasion, going to Luxemburg and Brussels, and even taking a trip to Stockholm, Sweden on one occasion in which he caught up with some of the athletes he competed with in the 1912 Olympics. It was also during this period that he began to take up hunting. It was the love of this simple pastime that would soon lead to General George S. Patton losing his life.

Chapter Ten

The Last Days of Patton

"How awful war is. Think of the waste."

—General George S. Patton

The above quote contains the words Patton had made just moments before a 2-ton military truck slammed right into the car that carried him, sending the General's body in the air and slamming his head against the thick glass partition that separated the back of his specially outfitted Cadillac from the front. His nose was smashed and his spinal cord severed in the violent collision, all in a matter of seconds.

As the wrecked car came to a halt and gravity brought Patton back to an upright position, his now completely numb body sagged and slumped to the side of its own accord. Patton knew that he was paralyzed, unable to feel anything from the neck down. In the backseat with him was his friend General Hobart Gay. Patton and Gay were out on a simple foray into the German countryside to hunt pheasants.

Now rendered paralyzed and completely helpless, in an instant General Patton now felt more like the hunted. Soon after the crash, an ambulance arrived on scene and rushed Patton to the newly established U.S. Army 130th Station Hospital. Upon arrival Patton's condition seemed to be rapidly deteriorating; the blood had drained from his face, and he was no longer responsive.

For the next two weeks, Patton would lay in a hospital bed with his upper body sealed in a plaster cast to decrease the horrible pressure on his spine while the hospital searched the world over for a neurosurgeon. The hospital staff finally settled on a U.S.-based expert in the field, Dr. Glen Spurling.

An all-points bulletin went out to track this neurosurgeon down, and it was soon discovered that he was on a train heading from Kentucky to Washington, D.C. Dr. Spurling was then intercepted in Cincinnati, and after being debriefed on Patton's condition was hastily flown out to see Patton.

However, in the end, all of these efforts would be in vain. General George S. Patton would pass away quietly on December 21st, 1945 of a pulmonary embolism a result of his weakened immobile condition. In a supreme irony, the General who all his life was so restless and full of energy passed away as a result of staying too still.

According to his wife Beatrice, who loyally sat by his side after being flown in from the United States, he succumbed to his injuries shortly after she read him a bedtime story. Patton loved being read to since he was a child; some say this was a product of his childhood dyslexia that had him craving others to read the spoken word that he sometimes struggled with.

At any rate, this was the last activity Beatrice would engage her husband with; after a few moments, he quietly informed her, "I'm getting sleepy. Why don't you go eat your dinner and we'll finish the chapter when you get back." Beatrice then obediently listened to her husband and went down to the cafeteria for her dinner while Patton went to sleep.

It was a sleep from which he would not wake up. Beatrice Patton was, of course, heartbroken, but the Patton family, long known for their penchant for the mystical, are said to have had a strange premonition even before their patriarch's injury occurred that he wouldn't be returning back to them after the war.

Patton himself alluded to these grim portents that he felt his "luck had run out" and he would be destined to die on the battlefield. Patton himself was a big believer in reincarnation, frequently alluding to past lives he had lived.

His daughter, Ruth Ellen, would later relate a story of waking up the morning of Patton's passing hundreds of miles away in the United States, only to see the old General standing right at the foot of her bed. She claimed that as soon as her eyes met his he simply smiled and faded away.

Whether we believe these anecdotal tales or not is rather arbitrary, but what can't be denied is that this larger-than-life and complicated American icon has a legend that will most certainly live on - in whatever shape or form it may be.

Conclusion

In recent years, much talk has been given about the idea that General Patton was assassinated due to his controversial and sometimes downright offensive beliefs. According to these conspiracy theorists, when the military truck slammed into Patton's Cadillac it was no accident but rather a clandestine hit, carried out by, well, just about anyone.

There were rumors early on that the Russian intelligence service wanted to take Patton out for his disparaging remarks against the Soviet Union and even as revenge for the way he treated some of the Russian generals. There is also speculation that Patton may have been purposefully bumped off by America's own military, which had been frowning upon Patton's behavior for quite some time.

Others allude to possible Nazi saboteurs; the list goes on and on. However, Patton's own family and friends (including those that were with him the day of the accident) have always maintained that they firmly believe that Patton's death was the result of an automobile *accident* and nothing more.

These declarative assertions from those closest to him have not been enough to silence conspiracy theorists, though, and the now endless books, such as Bill O'Reilly's "Killing Patton," and movies such as "Brass Target," which have endlessly speculated as to what the "true" cause of Patton's demise might have been.

For those who knew him best, the true cause was an automobile accident which caused a pulmonary embolism. Yet for those that seem to sense something much more dynamic, something more along the lines of a great Greek tragedy - for them, Patton was stabbed in the back by any number of possible Brutus'.

Made in the USA
Coppell, TX
13 February 2020

15635246R00028